To:

_____

From:

_____

Date:

_____

PAWFECT LOVE

♥ Life Is Best with a Love Like Yours ♥

Warren Photographic

ZONDERVAN

Pawfect Love
Text copyright © 2020 by Zondervan
Photography copyright © 2020 by Warren Photographic

This title is also available as a Zondervan e-book.

Requests for information should be addressed to:
Zondervan, *3900 Sparks Dr. SE, Grand Rapids, Michigan 49546*

ISBN 978-0-310-35413-0 (HC)
ISBN 978-0-310-45170-9 (e-book)

Art direction: Patti Evans
Interior design: Emily Ghattas

Printed in China

20 21 22 23 24 DSC 10 9 8 7 6 5 4 3 2 1

Contents

Introduction

Love is many things. It's the warm fuzzies we get when we hold someone's hand for the first time. It's the comfort in a mother's embrace. It's the warmth of a hug, the joy from a gift, and the butterflies we feel in a kiss.

But love is so much more than a feeling.

Love is kind. It causes strangers to extend goodwill. It brings communities together for a good cause. It leads spouses to forgive each other, and it reminds all of us, in every relationship, to give a second chance.

Love is forever. Even when we don't deserve it, true love sticks around. It doesn't ask us to be perfect. It sees us and knows us—warts and all—and says, "I love you. Always."

Love never fails. It heals our hearts and inspires us to take risks.

Most of all, love is shared. What's love, after all, if we keep it to ourselves? This doesn't mean relationships are easy or that you'll never get hurt. But the love you'll receive in return will make it all worthwhile.

Take a chance. Share your love with someone—with everyone—today. Like so many before you, you'll find that the real gift of love isn't found in what you're given but in what you're willing to give away.

One

Love Is
Kind

Let's be a comfortable couple, and *take care* of each other!

—Charles Dickens

11

I ask you to pass through life *at my side*—to be my second self, and best earthly companion.

—Charlotte Brontë

Remind me each morning of your *constant* love, for I put my trust in you.

—King David

Oh, the comfort—the *inexpressible comfort* of feeling *safe* with a person—having neither to weigh thoughts nor measure words, but pouring them all right out, just as they are, chaff and grain together; certain that a faithful hand will take and sift them, keep what is worth keeping, and then with the breath of kindness blow the rest away.

—Dinah Maria Mulock Craik

Love lifted me!

Love lifted me! When nothing else could help, love lifted me!

—James Rowe

Love has nothing to
do with what you are
expecting to get—only with
what you are expecting *to*
give—which is everything.

—Katharine Hepburn

Thy love is such I can no way repay; the *heavens* reward thee manifold, I pray.

—Anne Bradstreet

Love and the *gentle heart* are one same thing.

—Dante Alighieri

Be kind and compassionate to one another, *forgiving* each other, just as in Christ God forgave you.

—Saint Paul

Love, you know,
seeks to make
happy rather than
to be happy.

—Ralph Connor

Love is *friendship* that has caught fire. It is quiet understanding, mutual confidence, sharing and forgiving. It is loyalty through good and bad times. It settles for less than perfection and makes allowances for human weaknesses.

—Ann Landers

31

When you stop expecting people to be perfect, you can like them for *who they are*.

—Donald Miller

A loving heart is the *truest wisdom*.

—Charles Dickens

Love looks not with the eyes, but with the *mind*.

—William Shakespeare

What does love look like? It has the hands to help others. It has the feet to hasten to the poor and needy. It has eyes to see misery and want. It has the ears to hear the sighs and sorrows of men. That is what love looks like.

—Saint Augustine

Regardless of what else you put on, *wear love*.

—Saint Paul

Lord, grant that I might not so much seek to be loved as *to love*.

—Francis of Assisi

Two

―――――――――

Love Is Forever

When once I love, I love *forever*.

—Saint Thérèse of Lisieux

I know by experience that the poets are right: *love is eternal*.

—E. M. Forster

Choose love not in the shallows but in the deep.

—Christina Rossetti

All you need is love. But a little *chocolate* now and then doesn't hurt.

—Charles Schulz

Grow old along with me! *The best* is yet to be.

—Robert Browning

I love thee, I love but thee, with a love that shall not die till the sun grows cold, and the stars are old, and the leaves of the Judgment Book unfold!

—Bayard Taylor

The only way love can last a lifetime is if it's *unconditional*. And unconditional love is not based on how deserving the other person is, but rather on a choice to love them, no matter the circumstances.

—Stephen Kendrick

Most important of all, continue to show *deep love* for each other, for love makes up for many of your faults.

—Saint Peter

He is no lover,
who does not
love *forever*.

—Euripides

We love because it's the only true *adventure*.

—Nikki Giovanni

Love is not getting, but giving; not a wild dream of pleasure, and a madness of desire—oh no, love is not that—it is goodness, and honor, and peace, and pure living—yes, love is that; and it is the *best thing* in the world, and the thing that lives longest.

—Henry van Dyke

If a thing loves it is *infinite*.

—William Blake

Those who love *deeply* never grow old; they may die of old age, but they die young.

—Sir Arthur Wing Pinero

To love *abundantly*
is to live abundantly,
and to love forever
is to live forever.

—Henry Drummond

Gifts are temporary and often forgotten; love is forever and *always remembered*.

—Ken Poirot

Three

Love Never Fails

Love will *find a way.*

—Noble Sissle and Eubie Blake

The world's greatest *treasure* is a moment of shared love.

—Anonymous

One word *wipes out* all score of tribulations—love.

—Sophocles

True affection is *ingeniously* inventive.

—François Fénelon

Dear friends, let us love *one another*, for love comes from God.

—Saint John

Love *betters*
what is best.

—William Wordsworth

There is no *remedy*
for love but to
love more.

—Henry David Thoreau

Many waters cannot *quench* love; rivers cannot sweep it away.

—King Solomon

There is nothing holier, in this life of ours, than the first consciousness of love, the first *fluttering* of its silken wings.

—Henry Wadsworth Longfellow

What snag in life's plans cannot be *mended* by love?

—Anonymous

Most people live for love and admiration. But it is *by love and admiration* that we should live.

—Oscar Wilde

To love *deeply* in
one direction makes
us more loving
in all others.

—Anne Sophie Swetchine

I have for *the first time* found what I can truly love—I have found you.

—Charlotte Brontë

You're something
between a *dream*
and a *miracle*.

—Elizabeth Barrett Browning

When I think of what life is, and how seldom love is answered by love . . . ; it is one of the *moments* for which the world was made.

—E. M. Forster

The *single* desire that dominated my search for delight was simply to love and be loved.

—Saint Augustine

If there is *a little love*, the soul is comforted, the heart is softened.

—Saint Teresa of Ávila

'Tis better to have loved and lost than never to have loved at all.

—Alfred, Lord Tennyson

I will meet you again above, in that better land where there is no sin, no pain, no anguish, but where all is *light* and *love* and *immortality*.

—Wesley Bradshaw

Four

Love Is
Shared

Love unfolded naturally out of a *beautiful friendship*, as a golden-hearted rose slipping from its green sheath.

—Lucy Maud Montgomery

Strength lies in *differences*, not in similarities.

—Stephen R. Covey

From the first *moment* I beheld him, I was certain that on him depended the future happiness of my life.

—Jane Austen

When you really want love you will find it *waiting* for you.

—Oscar Wilde

He's more myself than I am. Whatever *our souls* are made of, his and mine are the same.

—Emily Brontë

Two souls with but a single thought, two hearts that *as one*.

—Harry B. Smith

All my heart is yours, sir: *it belongs to you*; and with you it would remain, were fate to exile the rest of me from your presence for ever.

—Charlotte Brontë

A great marriage is not when the "perfect couple" comes together. It is when an imperfect couple . . . learns to accommodate, and even *come to enjoy*, their differences.

—Dave Meurer

I do love *nothing*
in the world so
well as you.

—William Shakespeare

And then my soul saw you and it kind of went "*Oh there you are*. I've been looking for you."

—Iain S. Thomas

If ever two were one, *then surely we*. If ever man were loved by wife, then thee.

—Anne Bradstreet

To love at all is to be *vulnerable*.

—C. S. Lewis

What greater thing is there for two human souls than to feel that they are *joined for life*—to strengthen each other in all labor, to rest on each other in all sorrow, to minister to each other in all pain, to be one with each other in silent unspeakable memories at the moment of the last parting?

—George Eliot

Heaven comes down to touch us when we find ourselves safe in the heart of another.

—Mary Hollingsworth

I love thee to the *depth* and *breadth* and *height* my soul can reach.

—Elizabeth Barrett Browning

I have no notion
of loving people
by *halves*; it is
not my nature.

—Jane Austen

Love knows not
"mine" or "thine;" with
separate "I" and "thou"
free love has done,
for *one is both* and
both are one in love.

—Christina Rossetti

I never saw *so sweet* a face as that I stood before: my heart has left its dwelling-place and can return no more.

—John Clare

Notes

Notes are listed by page numbers.

Love Is Kind

10. Charles Dickens, *The Life and Adventures of Nicholas Nickleby*, vol. 2 (Leipzig: Bernhard Tauchnitz, 1843), 437.

12. Charlotte Brontë, *Jane Eyre: An Autobiography* (London: Service & Paton, 1897), accessed August 13, 2019, https://www.gutenberg.org/ebooks/1260.

14. Psalm 143:8 is taken from the Good News Translation in Today's English Version—Second Edition. Copyright 1992 by American Bible Society. Used by permission.

17. Dinah Maria Mulock Craik, *A Life for a Life*, vol. 2 (London: Hurst and Blackett, 1859), accessed August 13, 2019, https://www.gutenberg.org/ebooks/48482.

18. James Rowe, lyricist, and Howard E. Smith, composer, "Love Lifted Me," written in 1912, accessed August 13, 2019, from https://www.pdhymns.com/SheetMusic/Normal/I-Q/L/Love%20Lifted%20Me_N.pdf.

20. Excerpt from *Me: Stories of My Life* by Katharine Hepburn, copyright © 1991 by Katharine Hepburn. Used by permission of Alfred A. Knopf, an imprint of the Knopf Doubleday Publishing Group, a division of Penguin Random House LLC. All rights reserved.

22. Anne Bradstreet, "To My Dear and Loving Husband," Poetry Foundation, accessed August 12, 2019, https://www.poetryfoundation.org/poems/43706/to-my-dear-and-loving-husband.

25. Dante Alighieri, *The New Life*, trans. Dante Gabriel Rossetti (London: Ellis and Elvey, 1899), accessed August 21, 2019, https://www.gutenberg.org/ebooks/41085.

26. Ephesians 4:32 is quoted from the Holy Bible, New International Version®, NIV®. Copyright © 1973, 1978, 1984, 2011 by Biblica, Inc.® Used by permission of Zondervan. All rights reserved worldwide. www.zondervan.com. The "NIV" and "New International Version" are trademarks registered in the United States Patent and Trademark Office by Biblica, Inc.®

28. Ralph Connor, *The Major* (New York: George H. Doran Company, 1917), 249.

30. Excerpt from *Wake Up and Smell the Coffee!: Advice, Wisdom, and Uncommon Good Sense* by Ann Landers, copyright © 1996 by the Eppie Company. Used by permission of Villard Books, an imprint of Random House, a division of Penguin Random House LLC. All rights reserved.

33. Excerpt taken from *A Million Miles in a Thousand Years: What I Learned While Editing My Life* by Donald Miller. Copyright © 2009 by Donald Miller. Used by

permission of Thomas Nelson. www
.thomasnelson.com.

34. Charles Dickens, *David Copperfield* (London:
Bradbury & Evans, 1850), accessed August 21, 2019,
https://www.gutenberg.org/ebooks/766. Quote
adapted.

36. William Shakespeare, *A Midsummer Night's Dream*
(London: Simpkin, Marshall & Company, 1887), 11.

38. Saint Augustine, *The Confessions of St. Augustine*,
trans. E. B. Pusey, (London: J.M. Dent & Sons, Ltd.,
1907). Quoted adapted.

41. Colossians 3:14 is taken from *The Message*. Copyright
© by Eugene H. Peterson 1993, 1994, 1995, 1996,
2000, 2001, 2002. Used by permission of NavPress.
All rights reserved. Represented by Tyndale House
Publishers, Inc.

42. Francis of Assisi, "Make Me an Instrument of Thy
Peace," in *Prayers of the Middle Ages*, ed. J. Manning
Potts, (Nashville: The Upper Room, 1954), accessed
August 12, 2019, https://www.gutenberg.org/ebooks
/48242. Quote adapted.

Love Is Forever

46. Saint Thérèse of Lisieux (Thérèse Martin), *The
Story of a Soul: The Autobiography of St. Thérèse of
Lisieux*, trans. Thomas Taylor (London: Burns, Oates
& Washbourne, 1912), accessed August 22, 2019,
https://www.gutenberg.org/ebooks/16772.

48. E. M. Forster, *A Room with a View* (Mineola, New York:
Dover Publications, Inc., 2012), 166.

50. Christina Rossetti, "Cardinal Newman," in *Women
Poets of the Nineteenth Century*, ed. Alfred H. Miles,
(New York: E. P. Dutton, 1907; Bartleby.com, 2011),
accessed August 12, 2019, https://www.bartleby.com
/293/196.html. Quote adapted.

53. © Peanuts Worldwide LLC. Dist. By ANDREWS
MCMEEL SYNDICATION. Reprinted with
permission. All rights reserved.

54. Robert Browning, "Rabbi Ben Ezra," Poetry
Foundation, accessed August 12, 2019, https://www
.poetryfoundation.org/poems/43775/rabbi-ben-ezra.

56. Bayard Taylor, "Bedouin Song," in *The Little Book
of American Poets, 1787–1900*, ed. Jessie Belle
Rittenhouse (Boston: Houghton Mifflin, 1915), 127.

58. Alex Kendrick and Stephen Kendrick, *The Love
Dare Day by Day: A Year of Devotions for Couples*
(Nashville: B&H Publishing Group, 2013), 107. Used
by permission.

61. 1 Peter 4:8 is taken from The Living Bible. Copyright ©
1971. Used by permission of Tyndale House Publishers,
Inc., Carol Stream, Illinois 60188. All rights reserved.

62. Theodore William Alois Buckley, trans., *The Tragedies
of Euripides: Hercules Furens, the Troades, Ion,
Andromache, Suppliants, Helen, Electra, Cyclops,
Rhesus*, vol. 2 (New York: American Book Company,
1899), 70.

64. Nikki Giovanni, *Reader's Digest* (1982). Used by
permission.

66. Henry van Dyke, *Little Rivers: A Book of Essays in
Profitable Idleness* (New York: Charles Scribner's Sons,
1895), 114.

69. William Blake, *Complete Writings: With All the Variant
Readings*, ed. Sir Geoffrey Keynes (London: Nonesuch
Press, 1957), 91.

70. Sir Arthur Wing Pinero, *The Princess and the Butterfly*

(London: William Heinemann, 1897), 218. Quote adapted.

72. Henry Drummond, *The Greatest Thing in the World and Other Addresses* (Chicago: Fleming H. Revell Company, 1891), accessed August 21, 2019, https://www.gutenberg.org/ebooks/16739.

74. Used by permission of Ken Poirot.

Love Never Fails

78. Noble Sissle, composer, and Eubie Blake, composer, "Love Will Find a Way," Pathé Records, recorded August 29, 1921, accessed August 21, 2019, https://www.loc.gov/item/ihas.100010774/.

80. Anonymous.

82. Sophocles, *Oedipus at Colonus*, trans. F. Storr, Loeb Library Edition, (Cambridge, MA: Harvard University Press; London: William Heinemann Ltd., 1912), accessed August 13, 2019, https://www.gutenberg.org/ebooks/31.

85. François de Salignac de La Mothe-Fénelon, *The Spiritual Letters of Archbishop Fénelon: Letters to Men*, trans. H. L. Sidney Lear (London: Longmans, Green, and Co., 1914), 156.

86. 1 John 4:7 is quoted from the Holy Bible, New International Version®, NIV®. Copyright © 1973, 1978, 1984, 2011 by Biblica, Inc.® Used by permission of Zondervan. All rights reserved worldwide. www.zondervan.com. The "NIV" and "New International Version" are trademarks registered in the United States Patent and Trademark Office by Biblica, Inc.®

88. William Wordsworth, *The Poetical Works of William Wordsworth*, vol. 2 (London: Longman, Rees, Orme, Brown, Green & Longman, 1832), 162.

90. Henry David Thoreau, *The Writings of Henry David Thoreau*, ed. Bradford Torrey (New York: Houghton Mifflin and Co., 1906), 88.

93. Song of Songs 8:7 is quoted from the Holy Bible, New International Version®, NIV®. Copyright © 1973, 1978, 1984, 2011 by Biblica, Inc.® Used by permission of Zondervan. All rights reserved worldwide. www.zondervan.com. The "NIV" and "New International Version" are trademarks registered in the United States Patent and Trademark Office by Biblica, Inc.®

94. Henry Wadsworth Longfellow, *Hyperion and Kavanagh* (Boston: Houghton, Mifflin and Company, 1886), 190.

96. Anonymous.

98. Oscar Wilde, *De Profundis* (Berlin: S. Fischer Verlag, 1905), accessed August 13, 2019, https://www.gutenberg.org/ebooks/921.

101. Anne Sophie Swetchine, *The Writings of Madame Swetchine*, ed. Count De Falloux, trans. H. W. Preston (Boston: Roberts Brothers, 1869), 73.

102. Charlotte Brontë, *Jane Eyre: An Autobiography* (London: Service & Paton, 1897), accessed August 13, 2019, https://www.gutenberg.org/ebooks/1260.

104. Robert and Elizabeth Barrett Browning, *The Letters of Robert Browning and Elizabeth Barrett Browning*, vol. 1 (London: Harper & Brothers, 1899), 284. Quote adapted.

106. E. M. Forster, *A Room with a View* (New York: SDE Classics, 2018), 201.

109. Saint Augustine, *The Confessions of St. Augustine*, trans. E. B. Pusey, (London: J.M. Dent & Sons, Ltd., 1907), 21. Quoted adapted.

110. Saint Teresa of Ávila, *The Life of St. Teresa of Jesus* (London: Thomas Baker, 1904), accessed August 22, 2019, https://www.gutenberg.org/ebooks/8120. Quote adapted.

112. Alfred Gatty, *A Key to Lord Tennyson's "In Memoriam"* (London: George Bell and Sons, 1881), 30, accessed August 13, 2019, https://www.gutenberg.org/ebooks/36637.

114. Welsey Bradshaw, *Angel Agnes* (Philadelphia: Old Franklin Publishing House, 1873), accessed August 13, 2019, https://www.gutenberg.org/ebooks/17200.

Love Is Shared

118. Lucy Maud Montgomery, *Anne of Avonlea* (Canada: L.C. Page & Co., 1909).

120. From *The 7 Habits of Highly Effective People* by Stephen R. Covey. Copyright © 1989 by Stephen R. Covey. Reprinted with the permission of Simon & Schuster, Inc. All rights reserved.

122. Jane Austen, *Love and Friendship and Other Early Works* (1790), accessed August 12, 2019, http://www.gutenberg.org/ebooks/1212.

125. Oscar Wilde, *De Profundis* (Berlin: S. Fischer Verlag, 1905), accessed August 13, 2019, https://www.gutenberg.org/ebooks/921.

126. Emily Brontë, *Wuthering Heights* (New York: Harper & Brothers, 1858), 71.

128. Harry B. Smith, lyricist, and J. E. Hartel, composer, "Two Hearts That Beat as One," National Music Co., recorded 1890, accessed August 18, 2019, https://www.loc.gov/item/ihas.100006440/.

130. Charlotte Brontë, *Jane Eyre: An Autobiography* (London: Service & Paton, 1897), accessed August 13, 2019, https://www.gutenberg.org/ebooks/1260.

133. Dave Meurer, *Daze of Our Wives: A Semi-Helpful Guide to Marital Bliss* (Minneapolis, MN: Bethany House, 2000), 19–20. Used by permission.

134. William Shakespeare, *Much Ado About Nothing: Hudson's School Shakespeare* (Boston: Ginn and Heath, 1879), 118.

136. *I Wrote This for You* © 2018 Iain S. Thomas. Reprinted with permission of Andrews McMeel Publishing. All rights reserved.

138. Anne Bradstreet, "To My Dear and Loving Husband," Poetry Foundation, accessed August 12, 2019, https://www.poetryfoundation.org/poems/43706/to-my-dear-and-loving-husband.

141. C. S. Lewis, *The Four Loves*, copyright © C.S. Lewis Pte. Ltd. 1955. Extracts reprinted by permission.

142. George Eliot, *Adam Bede* (New York: Harper & Brothers, 1859), 491.

144. Mary Hollingsworth, *Just Between Friends: A Collection of Things Remembered* (Fort Worth, TX: Brownlow Publishing Co., 1995). Used by permission.

146. Elizabeth Barrett Browning, *Sonnets from the Portuguese* (New York: G.P. Putnam's Sons, 1902).

149. Jane Austen, *Northanger Abbey* (London: John Murray, 1817), accessed August 13, 2019, https://www.gutenberg.org/ebooks/121.

150. Christina Rossetti, "I Loved You First: But Afterwards Your Love," in *Poems* (Boston: Little, Brown and Company, 1906), accessed August 13, 2019, https://www.gutenberg.org/ebooks/19188.

152. John Clare, "First Love," in *Poems Chiefly from Manuscript*, accessed August 13, 2019, https://www.gutenberg.org/ebooks/8672.

About the Author

WARREN PHOTOGRAPHIC combines the artistic talents of Jane Burton and Mark Taylor, a mother-and-son team based in Surrey, England. Their work has been published in books and magazines, on greeting cards and calendars, and on a wide range of stationery and giftware. Many of the animals featured in their photographs are born and raised at the studio and have been introduced to each other and to modeling at an early age, allowing them to feel relaxed in each other's company on the set.